Let the Whales Escape

poems by

R. W. Haynes

Finishing Line Press
Georgetown, Kentucky

Let the Whales Escape

ACKNOWLEDGMENTS

The following poems were published in the journals listed. The author
thanks the various editors for their kind consideration.

Survivors, The Ghost from Stratford: *Ampersand Poetry Journal.*
Ibsen on the Nile: *Anastomoo* (originally "A Gift for Mrs. Ibsen").
John the Baptist Sings in the Shower: *The Broke Bohemian.*
No One Asked You to Volunteer: *Kritya.*
Ibsen's Spell: *The Muse—An International Journal of Poetry* (originally "The
        Homesick Norwegian").
Sonnet of the Two Pistols, Suzannah Lays It on the Table: *A New Ulster.*
Salto de San Antón: *Off the Coast.*
Light Late and Early: *Pocket Change.*
The Thracian Rider Is Doomed to Moonlight, Mona Lisa and the Marlboro Man:
        Poetry Life & Times.
To the Daughter of Light: *The Resurrectionist.*
That Flow: *Sage Trail Poetry Magazine* (originally "That Irresistible Flow of Words").
The Lost Poems of Catullus: *Sixers Review.*
Diogenes and Aristippus: *Sixty-Six: The Journal of Sonnet Studies.*
The Transmission of Artillery: *Sonnetto Poesia.*
On the Balcony of the Palacio de Cortés, *Concordia Discors* Paddles through the
        Swamp, On Ibsen's *Ghosts,* The Noble Roman, Vision and Code: *Tertulia.*
Devotion for Night: *whimperbang* (originally "Dark Devotion for Night").

Publisher: Leah Maines
Editor: Christen Kincaid
Cover Art: R. W. Haynes
Author Photo: Ruth Hernández Haynes
Cover Design: Elizabeth Maines McCleavy

Printed in the USA on acid-free paper.
Order online: www.finishinglinepress.com
        also available on amazon.com

Author inquiries and mail orders:
Finishing Line Press
P. O. Box 1626
Georgetown, Kentucky 40324
U. S. A.

Table of Contents

In loving memory of my parents:
William Leland Haynes
(1924-1987)
and
Sarah George Westbrook Haynes
(1925-1999)

Time Crumbles (And So Does Everything Else)

Time crumbles here in Galveston.
Undermined, the roots of memory
Give up and turn loose old slavery,
Bad old jokes which once were youthful fun.
That's that, then. Do you really mind
Tactful dilapidation creeping up
With its dead eyes and empty cup
As we review the colors of the blind?
Let it all go, as though the deadly tide
Were always here, as if the final terror hid
Till now, as if a golden age really did
Come and go, surge and then subside.
Come then and walk a while with me
As time crumbles finally into the sea.

A sane paranoia pervades this place
Where brute robs stupid brute and, profiting
From force, declares himself the rightful king
By gentle nature's adversarial grace.
These boasts and shows, at best ignored,
Often leave some hidden, peaceful space
Where we can dream and figuratively chase
Classic plans of sapient accord,
Yet in the mind at times there strangely flows
An instinct to sing war songs, to take a blade
And purge the nest these parasites have made;
So this violent mystery of raw nature glows,
And plans are pushed aside as violence draws
Our nature back toward our nature's laws.

Three-story card house…don't live there…
The stories build up a crushing weight and then
Everything falls, faces disappear,
And you either have to build once again
Or take your dim-lit wisdom elsewhere.
Cards may not be your game; if so,
Congratulations! That discovery

Should give you strength, for weaknesses you know
Often can be dealt with eventually.
Unnecessary games preserve a shallow
Imaginative realm for the naïve and callow,
Closing off a vast space of liberty.
The games we can and must not escape
Demand we put what wits we have in shape.

Hmm, observed Mr. Wittgenstein,
What's yours is yours, and what is mine is mine,
And both, I think, are in a sad decline.
My wife dropped me off at the Bulldog Inn
In hopes, perhaps, that I would display
More dignity when I emerged again,
Or possibly fortitude, who can say?
This conjecture faded from my thought
Before I was able to get very far,
For I pulled myself together and bought
A Colorado Bulldog at the bar,
Nectar for Hector, then, a splendid selection,
And an inward glow feeds my reflection
With sympathy, tolerance, and affection.

Schools of frightened fish skitter across
A distant fjord, and the yawning sun
Decides today will see no appreciable loss
Of cosmic loveliness, when all is done,
And deep, cold predators slash about
For satisfaction, staring eyes aglow
With natural instinct as the baitfish leap out,
Wild to flee the dreaded threat below.
A chain of connections of complexity
Resolves now in this light to simplicity
And all moves in this predictability.
Ha. And so we shiver, our gills in air,
Awaiting, frozen, whatever awaits us there.

Let the Whales Escape

Forgive us, Lord of swirling galaxies,
Conniptions, swaggers, hangnails, depression,
Noses bent awry by theories,
Goldfish behind glass; such secession
From gentle nature's decent dignity
Blocks imagination of giant whales
Spiraling downward in darkness forcefully
Driving light behind their sweeping tails.
It shuts down the springs where joy slowly flows.
It breaks us from our path to satisfaction,
Eliding our best hopes as blindness grows,
Baffling natural force with dull inaction.
Hope must keep its harmony and shape
As the mind imagines the great whales' escape.

Amado Nervo's Stone Head, Tepic, Nayarit, México

Imperative verbs, butterflies
Busily thinking of fluttering
And ducking like participles,
Slipping about like morphology,

Beneath the Great Stone Face
Of vastly detached apathy, which
Collects its dignity about itself,
Therewith better to loom.
Yes, there stands Amado like a stone wall.
There, but for the grace of granite.
There, you see, behind those morning glories.
There.

Feast Day of St Oláfr

I wish Emily Dickinson could see this.
I'm an old man crouched before a screen
In Laredo. To my left glows a scene
On another CRT, where northern light doth kiss
Weathered Norwegians preoccupied
With navigating where the huge fish hide,
Scooting fatalistically in mist of doom,
Vikings in motorboats, with baseball bills,
Plundering the depths, drowned in gloom
Contentedly among cold sloshes and swills.
That man in the blue jacket moors his boat
With such authority, but casually,
Caramba, madam, such a sight to see
Such dignity and disregard afloat,
O miraculous webcam, window on the fjord,
O bittersweet grace of the Lord!

From *A Faculty Handbook for the University of Rats*

"No one but poets should compose faculty handbooks."
– Ramón Fernández

O Rats, Don't Swim Toward that Sinking Institution

"John Connally is the only rat in history ever to swim toward a sinking ship."
– Sen. Tower

Admittedly, panic is not the best possible state
In which to contemplate the future or the past,
But some reactions just when the die is cast
Can save the prudent rat from cruel fate.
So you had thought that groveling before the dean,
A weighty rodent schooled in fragrant cheese,
In lies and crime astute and at his ease,
Would earn a place as a lackey Philistine.
Alas, the devil lies, and evil always thrives
By not being good, and these old rats
Laugh at the young and feed them to the cats,
And live at ease their long and vicious lives.
Though one is born a rat, one must not fail
To fear those beady eyes, that ratlike tail.

All Hell Fails to Break Loose on the Border

A slow day for news here in Laredo.
Things reported are just the things we know.
Let the heroes on television come and go.
All their diligent acting is just so-so.
"Full many a glorious morning" arrives here
Nudging mesquite and cactus, a prickly plain,
Thorns *dondequiera*, as if life were pain
For those unable to slither without fear.
Now for the sestet, lordings, a-one, two,
Justice requires something here, I believe…
A bit of syncopation to relieve
Insane expectation of something new.
In this desert staring hawks supervise
Raving lunatics screaming they are wise.

A Handy Form of Inertia

Steadiness, lonely virtue left alive
Not so inconvenient as to be
A vivid target for greedy eyes,
Lake-hogging swans, close friends
Closed now to friendship, moving on
To better arrangements. Brain cells die,
You see, and things change, obviously,
Leaving steadiness precious dignity,
Bobbing in the wake of novelty,
A hell of a deal on comedy.

Why say that I capitulated to
The forces of avarice and of that envy
Time let accumulate against me?
Was there something more heroic to do
Than ignore any advantages proposed
As well as the blustery intimidation?

The hot theater of self-identification
Cooled long ago, as fantasies, exposed
To the withering light of the noonday sun,
Surrendered to sanity; the vessel ran ashore,
Plunder exhausted, the magic sword I bore,
The last glowing force of desperation.
To organize for the last contention,
Is the last and best insanity prevention.

John the Baptist Sings in the Shower

As *new new new* gets old we hear the call
Forever crying for the newest stuff of all.
"Edgy," "avant-garde," et cetera, "Where's *BLAST*?"
Or even old Walt, whose self-publication
Defined the arrogance of a stupid nation
In the smug savagery of a Nazi past,
And blind and bigoted complacency
Dominates these cattle, so well-fed
On dumb ideas they moo the past is dead
But love old Ezra's demented agility
And reverence the wisdom of TV,
The self-reward of cleverness detached
From all experience of surfaces scratched,
And spin their squealing wheels obnoxiously.

An Internal Appreciation of the Swamp

This shadowed Okefenokee resounds
At night with overwhelming sympathy
Of moisture-loving creatures full of noise
And moved by dense familiarity,
In concordant croakery and clicks
Proclaiming their organic unity.

The ghostly heron navigates past
Beneath the heavy drapes of cypress fronds
And a hush touches the heart at last,
O quiet, frog-eating majesty.

Card Lesson in Deadwood

Wild Bill was always positioned for defense.
When he played cards, he would back his chair
Against the wall for safety. Common sense
Made it dangerous to attack him there.
Equally careful, I tended to place my bets
Within a tight defensive field of sight,
Expecting that all external threats
Would be reduced if supervised aright.
But then there are those grimmer threats within
That nullify this prudent attitude
And blind the warlike vision that has been
Safe, dissolving the defenses they delude.
Bill took a break from caution, foolishly;
So did I. The same thing happened to me.

On the Balcony of the Palacio de Cortés

Madness stands at one elbow. At the other
Various figures in masks take their turns,
And all whisper steadily, one after another,
Syllables whose content one never learns.
The maniac is familiar; one keeps a careful eye
On him night and day, and day and night,
But who are the others who are standing by,
And what are these advisements they recite?
I dream the lonely ghost of love is one
Whose only consolation is to speak of sin,
And when that sad companion is done,
I hear Complacency, Madness's mad twin.
I listen in patience, fighting back the fear
I'll never hear the voice I hope to hear.

Quetzalcoatl in Stone, Xochicalco

The guide tells us this sculpture commemorates
An intertribal congress that met to correct
Their remarkable calendar, and he stipulates
That the glyphs here specifically direct
The audience to that news. They also show
The incorrect data being corrected
And the marvelous power of the Maya zero
In shamanic communion. An unexpected
Voice laughs in my mind at this simple vision
Of handshakes and smiles, nodding colored plumes,
Delighted by this advance toward precision,
And Quetzalcoatl chuckles: "What this man assumes,
My friend, you had best ignore, or forget;
More when I return—but I haven't left yet."

Salto de San Antón

Cuernavaca, Morelos, México

I'm not dead yet. Listen to my voice
In this trashed-out canyon where I abide.
And this spirit's wild plunge filters inside
That part of the mind where sometimes you rejoice
And changes you forever in half-forgotten ways
So that the feathery neurons of your nervous being
See this cascade in their very act of seeing,
And quake, at times, at the phantoms I raise.
No, I'm not dead yet. My voice will be here
Forever, whatever else happens; these forces
Will operate; these irresistible courses
Will flow where they must, rushing dark or clear.
This song drives its melodious spell into
Droplets the Cuernavacan atoms renew.

Diogenes and Aristippus

Aristippus saw his philosophic rival
Washing down cabbages in the market place,
And, with a superior sneer on his face,
Remarked, "Diogenes, for financial survival
A man must accept a comfortable slavery.
Behold the difference between our positions."
"But what," asked the Cynic, "of our working conditions?
These good cabbages require no knavery.
If you were washing these vegetables here,
Instead of shamelessly flattering for pay,
You'd be as penniless as I am today,
But your wretched conscience might be clear.
I wash these cabbages, but my life is my own,
Your life is hostage to the tyrant on the throne."

Ibsen's Spell

When his Muse nudged him, Ibsen took
Down a poem, the essence of a play,
A melodic phrase that opened the gateway
Till he'd drawn all that power into a book.
He'd treasure these concentrated lines
As consecrated, an empowering spell,
A catalyst for concepts and character as well,
Invigorating the world the playwright defines.
And when the play was written out at last,
Then silently he'd set that spell afire,
And watch it curl, burn, and expire,
Its magic gone, now, into the past.
The play was born. Now Ibsen's pages
Flame forth dangerously on stages.

The Insurgency

The *taedium vitae* of single authority,
To sound true notes on long-neglected strings,
Tempts untried virtue with delectable things,
And by temptation brings dishonesty,
Canceling merit in motivation.
How then is this snooping quality
Better than a selfish debility
Despised by all as degeneration?
Let us calculate the abstractions here
And file them somewhere mentally,
Mutatis mutandis, where these thoughts will be
Convenient, available if needed, and clear.
Meanwhile, is there not a greater urgency
Gathering force, an imminent insurgency?

Survivors

The deafening pandemonium
Of war, its psychic shockwaves, shrieks and roars
Of human and inhuman conflicts which come
From the cacophonic martial harmonium
Give little rest or silence, calm or choice
To soldiers tense with agonized power
To listen for any still, small voice
Whispering wisdom in this distracted hour.
Yet the survivors, those who knew
A kind of grace in this chaos of force,
And who recall the tribute that is due
To fallen friends, compassionate remorse
And a kind of dedication, a gift from death,
Pause at times to listen, holding their breath.

The Ghost from Stratford

In Shakespeare's sonnets, a plain simplicity
Fences with its opposite, a complex vision,
More narrow, more conscientious in decision,
Wiser, feebler, with a more prudent clarity,
Cooler, inept to wrest the loosened reins
From demented passion in emergencies,
Safer to trust—when one must—but a disease
To all the satisfactions it detains.
It is the other which concerns us most,
Of course, for here it comes, that fog of sorts
That engages, enrages, tantalizes, contorts
The prepared identities we used to boast
Were integrated parts of our destined roles,
And passionate destiny shoots them full of holes.

The Transmission of Artillery

My father, aged 20, was seriously wounded by German artillery fire near Metz, November 20, 1944.

It's been with me always, this dream of hell,
Of cannon fire which shakes the ground and makes
A vertiginous nightmare, shrapnel and earthquakes
And no good place to hide from the next shell.
I remember clearly how you used to tell
Lightly, but with a strange look on your face,
How when a shell explodes the only place
To jump is in the smoking crater where it fell,
As though that were a precious fact your sons
Might one day need, as you did in France,
At twenty, as Hitler's cannons made you dance
For life under fire from those great guns.
I hold in my heart this share of your anxiety,
The part of your nightmare you passed on to me.

A Voice from Annapolis

A kind of quiet glory does at times pervade
A profession both embattled from outside
And from its own quislings, those who've played
Their cards simply for the cash they hide.
We imagine the wry smiles, the shaking heads,
Of all our legendary professors' ghosts,
Perceiving our universities now as hotbeds
Of ignorance, pandemonium, the latest outposts
Of progress from university to fools' empire.
Jacob Klein once spoke, as always, quietly,
And said, "I believe there is nothing higher,"
And paused, "than intellectual activity,"
And that voice persists, despite the condition
Of the university, a reminder of mission.

An Experienced Commander

An experienced commander of a ragtag force
Approaches combat with a wise trepidation.
So I arrange this and that high-risk resource
To secure an objective, but with reservation
That if that or this one abandons a station
A hasty reinforcement or safe escape
Will prevent a collapse or an annihilation
And assure survival in some kind of shape.
Yet in this seasoned skillfulness of mind
A fearful prospect sometimes undercuts
The urge to outwit the enemy and find
A victory: this dark mood suddenly puts
Everything at risk. This subversive deceit
Confounds all intention, threatening defeat.

Light Late and Early

The light at sunrise and that at end of day
Glows with a generous quality that suffuses
The world with a depth that light loses
As the sun ascends, shadows dwindle away,
And the harder edges of the things we see
Then claim their differentiating worth,
And all visible objects upon the earth
Stand apart and sing of their own integrity,
Until the angle of the sun declines again
And that generous quality of light returns
To bless and forgive as the quiet sun burns
Ever less fiercely in its decelerating spin
Toward China. Between the darkness of night
And blameful noon, let us live in angled light.

No One Asked You to Volunteer

No one asked you to volunteer
To be cannon fodder in the war against lies,
But you saw for yourself there was no clear
Alternative. So then one tries and dies?
Sometimes that's it, but then, on occasion,
The charge breaks through the fortified lines
Of stupidity, puts to rout prevarication,
And rips down hypocrisy's posters and signs;
The guilty are punished, justice is done,
The just are rewarded, a sweet harmony
Resounds on the field where the battle was won,
And hope smiles on a noble victory.
The victors put aside their weapons and take up
The implements of peace, and then you wake up.

The Obscurity of Clear Purpose

We have spring mists even in Laredo, and when
Huge banks of fog pervade the cactus and mesquite,
Improbability seems so inevitable, then,
As if there were no tyranny of heat.
Our sculptured plans, which budget all emotion,
Dismiss their Spartan clarity when those
Humid clouds roll in; the stealthy notion
Of solace slyly sprouts and grows.
Noble renunciation finds itself renounced
And put aside; the blooming mental flowers
Of spring exclaim aloud that they have trounced
Quiet self-control, their vividness is ours.
And I put a careful marker in my book
And put it down, and look for your look.

The Eraser

In the morning silence on the battleground,
The waste and wreckage does no more than say
That force met force in violence yesterday.
Nothing remains to tell what victory was found
Or what disappointment happened here,
And those who lived can celebrate the win
Or bitterly bemoan what might have been,
But today a single mockingbird sings clear
Where passions clashed in force the day before.
And my mind is blank; I have no sympathy
For either side; though one of them to me
Was kin, that kinship is for me no more.
Now there is no partisanship or choice,
Only the warble of this mockingbird's voice.

The Noble Roman

Cassius: *Did Cicero say any thing?*
Casca: *Ay, he spoke Greek.*

In the *De Officiis* of Marcus Tullius Cicero
No doubt there is some eloquent *locus*
Showing forth like a new-sprung crocus
The reasons I ought already to know
For abiding this challenge, forsaking verse,
Filling my mind with officious detail,
Deadening my mornings with travail,
Oblivious to Mephistopheles' curse.
But Tully himself never did so very well
As when, kicked from office, he composed
Himself in the history he then supposed
He was missing in his ostracized hell.
O Cicero, you did your duty best
When you abandoned it, under protest.

Chaucer at Iwo

It is the inadequate side of the mind that makes
Little islands into hells of brutality,
Emulates Nature's mutual munching and takes
On none of its flower-shaping spirituality.
This ignorance is nobody's bliss, for strife
Contrary to wisdom generates misery,
And poses great peril for the philosophic life,
As does your willful ignorance of me.
This distracted air is a dog-eat-dog device,
The more so if it is unintended,
And that half-courteous smile produces ice
Where Zephyrus and my blood are blended.
One day may a better nature take control
And take the Iwo Jima in my soul.

That Flow

That irresistible flow of words recklessly
Generating its own essential momentum and plot
And gushing gravitationally in what must be
A modestly fatal dialogue, but, perhaps not,
Perhaps it is instead a dash for liberty,
And in its reckless progress a virtue shows,
And breathless desperation to be free
Excites immoderation as it grows
Apace and uncontrolled, nearly mindlessly,
Until the need for silence grows so great. . .
That flow of words, I say, my own biography,
Accelerates toward silence, a riddling state
Where motion of mind is escape velocity,
And no matter then what velocity I find,
It only serves to leave me more behind.

Faction Threatens

Faction threatens to disintegrate
The body politic, but deliberation,
Says Hamilton, can moderate
That prospect of disintegration.
Walking past the Hamilton Hotel,
Returning from Mexico once again
To Laredo, I wonder if he considered well
What this body would experience in
The coming years, what it would go through,
Whether deliberation would be a sufficient
Remedy for malice developing anew
Where elusive dialogue emerges deficient.
If time tries truth, let this seasoned solution
Stabilize our centrifugal revolution.

Wake to Escape

Breaking through the thin ice of behavior
And floundering, shocked, in the icy bath
Of galvanized imbecility, no savior
Ready to pull one back to the path
Of righteous sleep-walking in a tempest unseen
Or to erase those magical maledictions
One casually pronounced, O glib Philistine,
Annihilating all of one's convictions.
So how to escape? If one merely lies
To escape the truth, he will not extricate
Himself from the penalty his act implies,
Nor will mere metaphor extenuate
The circumstances of his hapless break-up.
Wake up and live. Come to life. Wake up.

Ophelia on Self-Pity

Self-knowledge, then, is to be sought,
While self-pity is put aside, disdained
With other vanities our pilgrimage has taught
Debilitate us, left unrestrained.
The latter, though, stealthily gratifies
While the former perpetually deletes
Satisfaction as it fiercely satisfies
Itself by purging the pleasures it defeats.
Is it true, then, that this duality
Dominates, my spirit, our contemplation?
Or are these eddying currents in a sea
Of random, sporadic, neural agitation?
Self-knowledge saves us from ignorant shame
When self-pity and it are not the same.

Night on Oslo Harbor

One sets out to set so many things right,
Stimulated by the value of what goes well,
And many an excellent thing comes to light
From virtuous vigor resolved to excel.
Somehow the evaporation of honest sweat,
However, leaves a toxic residue behind
To turn good purpose to ill and set
Dementia awork in an energetic mind.
When Ibsen returned to this distressing theme,
He understood how his Norwegian Muse
Stood uncertain in this nightmarish dream,
Its power a power both to gain and lose,
Resolved to escape that end against the wall
Where iconoclasm is the worst icon of all.

Johnie Armstrong Arrives from the Office

When a battle seems to end, and all the dead
Are buried, homeward, eventually, go the rest
To battle forever forth in nightmares instead
Of on the field where death did its best.
And, instead of enemies shooting to kill,
They go forth to face a fiercer adversary,
The Machiavellian armed with a quill,
Empty of spirit, but, on the contrary,
Full of malicious and ignorant spite,
Determined to make all blessed work cursed,
To block all excellence from coming to light,
And to represent all the best work as the worst.
This creature makes certain that conflict never ends;
The war is never over. Fight on, my friends.

Ibsen on the Nile

Those monuments are monuments merely
Of themselves; this river of nutrition
And death, inundating Egypt, is clearly
A muddy embodiment of time's volition.
I saw the Sphinx off in the distance. Today
I purchased an ancient mummified hand
To give to my wife, safely far away,
And I suspect that she will understand.
I met DeLesseps recently. He and I
Have much in common, more than he knows;
My work is lonelier, but there exists a tie
Between what we do as humankind grows.
These monuments record the vanity of ages;
Mine put the outraged human soul on stages.

Thank You for the Note

Negotiating past the ruin, I see the past
And future fused, the various vanities
Of desire and hope hopelessly cast
Inextricably tangled with these
New obstacles; recognition
Mirrors reconciliation,
And emerging afresh, volition
Feeds fresh life to negotiation,
And, as in music, all moves ahead
Majestically toward consummation
In a final burst of noise, and dead
Silence deathlily pauses all creation.
Thank you for the note. Such notes are, to me,
The trophies of this aimless odyssey.

Don't Forget the Tickets

Reluctantly confronting the necessities of age,
Retreating with what one can desperately
Collect, recalling moments that lit the page
With glorious recognition, thriftily
Packing essentials tightly for the trip,
Putting aside nonsense, an easier task
Now than in that long apprenticeship
Of farewells, knowing, now, what questions to ask,
We manage cash and maps, papers, keys,
Food, shelter, clothing, the perennial needs,
The whole host of details, shepherding these
Toward the exit to which everything leads.
Somehow we assemble the baggage clumsily,
Look at each other, laugh uncontrollably.

Ibsen Misses the Ocean

"What I most miss here is the sight of the sea. . ."
Ibsen

It takes a long time for a ship to make its way
Along a winding fjord and to arrive,
Or return to the horizon after long delay
And lingering memories keeping hope alive.
This is Norway. The ships come and depart
As dreamily laden once as they still glide
With hopes, gold, slaves, passions of the heart,
Domestic aspirations, tourists for the ride,
And brooding eyes still watching from the shore
Where home-bound Vikings once watched enviously
As the dragon ships plunged forth and headed for
Rich plunder southward down the murderous sea.
The fjord is the portal of long deliberation,
Fantasy, acceptance, and renunciation.

Benediction, Valediction

Let us give thanks for these courtesies
Of this famous emotion, and, crumbling
Minimally, if cringing at bit at these
Half-faced cordialities, stumbling
Somewhat in this stately pantomime
Comprising grinning, mindless puppetry—
The old cold cell looks better all the time:
Its narrow window facing the cold sea—
Here we are, the artificial light
Enchantingly generating sleight of hand
Like opium dreams, inflecting the right
Poised and subjunctive glances on command.
With so little strength delivered from the heart,
We have the more energy left to depart.

Sonnet of the Two Pistols

Her shining Beretta and his battered .38
Lay together on the nightstand side by side.
Guardians of this unsanctioned date,
Suspending detonation to abide,
Romantic souvenirs of hopeful protection
(Hers a graduation present to assure
A daughter's safe commencement, his selection
A museum piece of origin obscure).
Both fully loaded, carefully maintained,
Safety locks poised for sudden release,
Faithful companions whose company sustained
Passion, guaranteeing momentary peace.
And later, the lady, something seeming wrong,
Hid them under pillows where they belong.

The Cycle of Escape

Twelve months ago today I fought a vicious fool
And his demented and destructive friends,
And all my power resisted his misrule.
Today that excruciating injury mends:
I turn to a better purpose that intends
To leave these squealing, clawing apes behind
In hell where their contention never ends,
Nor their annihilation of the mind,
Turning away, resolute to find
A worthy value in philosophy,
And, if not final peace, at least a kind
Of cleanness, if I find no tranquility
Manifests itself, a hygienic sanity
Removed from that ferocious vanity.

The Puppet Possesses

The puppet possesses no integrity,
Of course, its function only to display
Or conceal its master's ingenuity,
An empty instrument convenient for today,
Perhaps, and tomorrow to be put away.
The nullness of this thing, and its pretense
Of responsibility, invites us to say,
We deluded members of the audience,
"Explain your part in this painful play,"
But there's nothing there, a painted grin
And eyes of glass: the master's gone away.
Garbage is left; this character caves in.
A masterless puppet has nothing to say.

The Poet as Fisherman

Since you must be caught to get away,
Be alert always for the golden hook
Concealed in the pages of this book,
Though you have been landed anyway,
In the broken moment's perception
Which marks the fisherman's jealousy
And never articulately intends to be
More mere gesture than deception.
Know you suddenly will be told
Something unbearable, with fatal precision,
Paralyzing both perception and decision,
A little death to all the life you hold.
The surface erupts, but the struggling prize,
The fish, has the fisherman's eyes.

Judas Looks at His Watch

"What is truth?" one asks, and washes one's hands
Of the past, as though in fact that could be done.
But the ice is thin wherever one stands
Surrounded by the ghosts of everyone
One has washed one's hands of, all outraged
And vengeful, some because rejection
Was just, others just because upstaged
By distraction, neglect, or a new connection,
And some grossly betrayed, staring in pain,
Their wide eyes asking, "How? *Cómo?* How?"
Demanding that one impossibly explain
One's unbelievable dereliction now.
So one shrugs them off, trying not to think
How those thirty pieces of sweet silver clink.

The Consolation of Inconsolability

If you dismiss this cruelty from your mind
Awhile, and focus on what has been tried
To make you happy, perhaps you'll find
A comfort which impatience has denied
Which calls more for awareness than disdain,
Although confusion dominates you now,
And anger, and that outrageous sense of pain,
Furiously shrieking, "How can this happen? How?"
And all the standard words of consolation
Can rain upon your agony constantly,
Not diminishing your devastation
Unless you end your vulnerability.
No platitudes can console you very well,
Though life is war, and we know war is hell.

A Rule of Detection

There can be ceremony even within
The scrupulous avoidance of each stage
Of a recognized ritual, and thus I begin
With a strangled smile, suppressed outrage,
To counterpoint possibly predictable paces,
But, bowing inwardly to this demented dance,
Curse the grins on all our guilty faces,
And kick out my feet, and caper, and prance.
For rules are rules, even when encoded,
And masks on masks are usually required
For both the predators and the devoted,
For both the envious and the inspired.
Let then our rule of detection be
To turn a blind eye to the masks we see.

Concordia Discors Paddles through the Swamp

I have not forgotten how blithely to deny
Or to abandon, although neither of these
Abuses is sufficiently decent to justify
Its tyrannical interpolation to appease
The small *demonios* of convenience,
And thus I perpetuate this conversation
On tenterhooks amid vague fingerprints,
Disturbing recollections of old sensation,
Half-desperate glances at watches and at faces.
We put in the boat at sunrise, hopeful echoes
Of birds haunting the launch with whistling graces,
With swirls astern as our good ship goes,
And sudden excitement as one madly lunges
As her bobber suddenly plunges.

To the South Texas Moon

O moon, vilified for inconstancy,
Will no one remember that law of gravity
Gravely methodizing your lunacy,
O paradigm of obedient punctuality?
The path of high words leads to misery,
For, in truth, this low sublunarity
Confers on pride no authority,
And the harder path of humility
Can baffle all ingenuity.
Yet we mock the physical certainty
Of your tide-changing regularity,
Knowing that, when our vanity
Is forgotten, your light will be
Blessing our desperate posterity.

South of Sofia

Prudence requires motives. In the confusion
Of what makes us fox-trot through this wood
Of wary weariness, unending profusion
Of alternatives, none of them any good,
We look for the heavens to show the way,
And there between the concealing leaves
May lie a fragment of Lyra to obey,
But, otherwise, conjecture persuades and deceives.
So prudence requires prudence, it cannot begin
In imprudence. Insanity may well smirk
At sanity, but it won't let it in,
Nor will caution let incaution do its work.
This howling darkness of occluded skies
Requires wisdom to philosophize.

Each Other's Faces

Another dark lady wrote the paper on waiting.
Another sonneteer shook the clouds with doom.
And this tedious, overstated, form of understating
Does not defy the echoes in this room.
You threw that mask of Medusa to the floor
With fine dramatic power but ostracized,
Alas, an epic personality that came no more
And left that sword-drawn hero paralyzed.
Suppose we defy defiance, thinking back,
With at least a shattered mask, poems scrawled
And read furiously, lest coherence should attack,
Remnants memory has dementedly recalled,
Assigning passion a precious place of places,
Passionately obliterating each other's faces.

Reflect and Prepare

If we cannot forgive each other for what we did,
Let's not do it either for what we did not do.
You traded slaves until you had hid
A fortune; I hit the rough life, black and blue
From hard nights and useless washed-up days,
But there was a kind of truth beween us two
That galvanized laughter, attraction always,
If rueful, appreciative, all the days we knew.
And, cruel as those times sometimes were,
Even crueler is the intrusive thought
That that was all, and our present will refer
Perpetually to that reckless past we brought
Upon ourselves unthinkingly. Now perhaps
We know to avoid those unavoidable traps.

The Path by the Border

They hate us youth!
Sir John Falstaff

It is sometimes good to forget, although
Oblivion, the last antagonist, reminds
Us always of the river Lethe's flow,
And now that the young mind rarely finds
Joy in anything surviving from the past,
Except hedonism, sloth, and illiteracy,
Deep regrets when sunrise comes too fast,
Eternal things escaping cruel maturity,
We walk in silence, sometimes hand in hand,
Surrendering these sweet angels of remorse,
As ducks fly past us over the Rio Grande,
And the darkening sun diminishes its force.
"Well, we did that, too," we may remark,
Half-proud, half-sorry, in half-gloomy dark.

Still, Small Voice from the Burning Bone-House

A cautiously quiet response to the pressure of lies
Is best, no doubt, and who can find fault
With prudence? The wisdom on which one relies
For safety against the virulent assault
Of treachery, protective coloration,
Patience, judicious eye contact, restraint
In even the most casual conversation
With never a commitment or complaint. . .
That's fine; I can't ask that this holocaust
Of conscience and consciousness extend
Beyond its proper bounds, that you exhaust
Your security options because a friend
Has a problem, that in your safe complacency
You entertain this insanity.

Pound at the Keyboard

"Pish for thee, Iceland dog! Thou prick-eared cur of Iceland!"

"Cry havoc and let slip the dogs of war. . ."

Even though Homer never had to type
With a Schnauzer puppy wriggling in his lap
Attacking the keys with vicious pounce and snap,
And Vergil must have had slaves to wipe
All the teardrops up from the floor
Before his dogs could lap those tears,
Lacrimae rerum for the struggling years,
Like the blood of heroes alive no more—
Ah, those would be salty dogs indeed,
(This one, plunging for the Escape key,
Requires Shift, Ctrl-Hold the puppy)
To slurp what those old soldiers bleed—
I say. . . what was it? Did those old bards
Succeed by keeping their dogs in their yards?

Kermit and Miss Piggy Chat on the Balcony

We strode the seas and made the barricade
Of language so strong that only pure silence
Could call itself poetry in the world we made,
Vaulting like cartoons, resonant in violence,
Fabled powers charging gesture and gaze,
Generating drama transfixing the mind,
Moving toward the ultimate gesture always,
The devastating sideways look, the refined
But spontaneous, sudden half-raised hand,
The kiss more thought than ever, ever kissed;
The thunderbolt of reproach, to demand
A silent annihilation, never missed.
These swarming monstrous memories engage
Us so. How do we get off this stage?

The Dogs of the Mind Bark at the Door Bell

"thou hast the strength of laws. . ."
Sonnet 49

Separation is the word that comes to mind
Each time enough distractions have ceased
To allow its return, one coldly left behind,
The other left untethered, just released
From all connection except when I
Acknowledge the long-contested discovery
That, lo and behold, poetry will not deny
An unseen bond but instead, impatiently free,
Will protest, impel, urge, outrageously demand
The case in writing, stated quietly
With careful, woeful words that justly understand
Connection in separation, and in turn,
How to connection separation must return.

As Lighter Wights Turn Loose

These weights have places, times, and destinies.
Thoughtless damage is done by reckless shifts
Crudely moved by the mind that drifts
Toward its visions of voluptuous ease.
So this vocation is not a vacation,
Nor this burdened life a search for careless rest,
Or a dream of self-indulgence, a hapless quest
For absolute exoneration.
The balance is precise on this thin ice,
But this substantial sustenance sustains,
Before temptation's ambivalent pains,
The lovely music, the click of the dice:
This familiar burden lets me stay
As lighter wights turn loose and blow away.

On the Ambivalent Security of Abstraction

And over al this, yet muchel more he thoughte
What for to speke, and what to holden inne. . .
Troilus and Criseyde I.386-387

The backwash of ambivalence supplies
A kind of baffled chorus to recognition,
Rushing to distract with a flood of half-lies,
Babbling quietly in shallow inanition.
Yet what has most marked the moments before,
Ceteris paribus, the flare in the night,
The long-awaited turning of the key in the door,
The furiously oxidizing meteorite,
The consummation of a sympathetic glance,
Defies the foolish chorus's afterthought,
Separating essence from the circumstance
And grasping the value the recognition brought.
Thus abstractly, here in darkness I review
The painful wisdom of yesterday anew.

Walter Gordon Leaves Indiana

The conversation graduates now,
And when I read to you yesterday
"Take no thought of your life," somehow
Those words had been realized anyway.
You were the priest, after all, despite
It all. No priest or poet is complete
Without some visionary insight
That practicality cannot defeat.
Yet here I was, reading St. Matthew
To the telephone someone held by your ear,
"Behold the fowls of the air," and you
Tried to speak as though you could hear.
The conversation graduates; we made
It through the course. Sir, what is my grade?

Aphrodite of a Prufrock

He didn't quite believe that Aphrodite
Was as devious and ferocious as reputed,
But he observed stealth in case her mighty
Power might just in case be thereby muted.
But he *had* always thought that time was on his side,
Which was true, but not quite in the sense
He thought it was; that slippery slide
Answered a different gravity; his defense
Was strong but mislocated; one can fight
The elements longer when one is not so blind.
Miscalculating prudently without insight
Makes for familiar distress of the mind.
So he glanced and grimaced, carried on,
Unable to smother the occasional moan.

The Expiration Date

Your pity and my disappointment will expire
Simultaneously, the fading cries of crows
At sunset, burnt by surreptitious fire,
Washed away like heartbroken echoes.
And that's fine and dandy, sports fans,
For in this bower of bliss the greatest force
To learn is that force which nothing bans,
Nothing debilitates or denies recourse,
For the eloquence of silence, deriving strength
As the quiet oak collects its dignity,
Sustains a gentle autonomy at length
Empowering patience and durability.
Disappointment teaches, despite our fears,
Its last lesson: disappointment disappears.

The Psalms of Consolation

In weariness the psalms of consolation
Connect the texture of truth and delightful feel,
A kind of righteously hedonistic sensation
With satisfying infusions of harmony to heal,
And quietly to recognize how, eventually,
Discord, delay, and cruel disconnection
Yield to their opposites, and a maturity
Of comprehension clarifies connection.
So here we are, and these foolish grins
Betray a future where all will be well
And sweet psalms' true resonance begins,
And truth is told that now no one can tell.
The desperate confusion that now seems to reign
Conceals its sanity, seemingly insane.

Another Good Friday

If a grain of gold compassion falls
To titanic depths, crushed by the sea
In a nameless place no human mind recalls,
And, in my busy life, I fail to see
How that lost promise, found, should be
The radiant center of my universe,
Then I am in that darkness, never free
From that crushing, unspeakable curse.
And, on my own, a blind debility
Constrains me to stumble in confusion,
Except when, sometimes, I suddenly
Find illumination replacing illusion.
And then that merciful magnitude
Annihilates my ineptitude.

A Song of the Nueces

Clear water, its own symbol, its representation
Transparent in words and its cleansing
Refreshment a marvelous condensation,
Irrigates, hydrates, perpetually rinsing,
Delightful in motion, in music, cascading
And splashing in shallows on rocks,
And in deep repose always accumulating
The force of life, a majestic paradox.
Thus the symbol. According to St. Paul,
The letter killeth but the spirit giveth life,
And, to change the saying, we spoil it all
In sophisticating overmuch; this strife
Begins when we lose that transparency
Clear water and common wisdom let us see.

This Storm

"Out of the south cometh the whirlwind. . ."

As the blasts of brainlessness dissolve into inaction
And passion for the neat replaces passion of the heart,
So the formula becomes the *telos,* satisfaction
The completion of the algorithm, and art
A pedantic footnote to technology.
So here in our house, the academy,
Once the temple of high philosophy,
Vile politicians flourish in villainy,
And wisdom, like King Lear, in the storm outside
Shrieks for justice, while those who care,
Destitute themselves, desperately abide
In hope of mercy in the devastating air.
Peace, then, for tormented, passionate souls
Whom, in this storm, this violent evil controls.

Boarding the Stage

Eloquence having missed its path again,
Some show of credibility will have to do,
Though show, to those who know, will win
Few converts, even when the show is true.
And to an audience of one, chosen of all
For omniscient eye and remorseless mind,
Show must show well not to recall
Half-forgotten things, elsewhere assigned.
And if the game is worth the candle, then,
One must step forth on the stage and pronounce
The fatal words, and make those faces again,
And sigh, and shrug, and tragically renounce.
Letting the hand fall, thus, rejecting delight,
Devoutly avowing rightness of the fall of night.

The Words Do Not Perish

The words do not perish; as mystery
They sustain, for they both speak
When spoken and abide infinitely
As does that infinite love we seek.
Parents live in the prayers they moan
For their children wandering in perilous places,
Prayers which return when the children are grown
And have forgotten their dead parents' faces,
With quiet power urging them, now, to pray
For those whose sensual pleasures prevail
But who will, chastened, need those words one day,
And may find, then, that love does not fail.
Words in darkness, fear, and anxiety,
Addressed aright, must shape fidelity.

This Cat for Sale

Since they put his face on the cat food sack,
My cat has experienced discontent,
Sometimes wanting to take his picture back,
For he lost some independence when it went.
Now his neat countenance, white and black
Proclaims to all the meretricious theme
That he has become a lackey and a hack
And a slave of the commercial American dream.
If good cat food is for good cats indeed
And good cats know exactly what they crave
As well as the few things they really need,
Why advertise a product? O base slave,
Hast thou diminished thine integrity
And dost thou now reflect remorsefully?

The Consolation of Don Roberto Crumb

She left with Hungry Chuck Biscuits, leaving
Him twisting in his creative hurricane
Where the quiet eye left him conceiving
That words water the spirit like rain.
And when the dawn came up he walked
Toward the sun on a red-clay Georgia farm,
Forgiving madly; all alone he talked
To mockingbirds and thrashers; he knew no harm
Was done. He knew the weather had to change
And that expedient Alka-Seltzer affections
We have fiercely strained our prudence to arrange
Dissolve instantly in all directions
At the touch of the elemental. She and Chuck
Plopped and fizzed, but left the poet luck.

Walking Down the Hall, Gasping

Fairly fragmented, yet undismayed,
Still feeling one's way toward a final code
Which seems to lie around that sixth decade,
Mirages receding on this deserted road,
The diffidence of inexperience evaporates
In the heat of familiar exertion,
And a kind of killer instinct habituates
The heart to both highway and desertion.
That's the good news, and, on the other hand,
The ship is sinking, the cat is afire,
The marbles rolling madly to beat the band,
And as the sky is falling it gets higher,
And focus escapes its accustomed grasp
With each unaccustomed mental gasp.

Ditty for the Barbarians

Awake from this dream? Ha. Into what
Awaken? Where ideas normally distort
And processed bias passes for thought but
Remains a subtle nightmare where demons sport
And the dream taken for wakefulness goes
As its lethal vigor unconsciously grows?
Give me the right kind of power saw,
And I'll shape something that I think will do:
Flying chips and sawdust snarling through
Deadwood and dumbness—here's the law,
You zombies, force, racket, brutality
Will wake you up—your stupid eyes will see
Death has you by your cringing, twitching brain…
And that's that, assholes. Stop reading now.
I charge by the word for both jackass and cow,
And if you squeeze your wallet any worse
It may explode and waste this drowsy curse.

Was There Something Else?

I don't know. Was there? Maybe in
The tone of voice. Maybe in the striking way
Those two ducks turned into the chilly wind,
And there was nothing else, then, to say.
It does no good to go through this again
Unless, somehow, a smiling angel hid
And giggled at the eloquence of sin,
But knew there was no harm in what we did.
Is that what it was? If so, we'll think again
And probe the various possibilities,
For grace will have its way, no question then,
When feelings feebly fall upon their knees.
The hamster wheel of wisdom strikes again…
No more questions. Make the treadmill spin.

Sacred Vessels Hover in the Mist

Boats of the spirit, speaking murmurously
Of ancient tides and always-threatening shoals,
Turbulent passages of moonlit opportunity,
Calm voyages of quiet philosophy,
Strengthening for when the heavy weather rolls,
Tethered at the venerable pier, you shift
As if awakened by the turning sun
To browse the light among experienced friends,
A bump of shoulder, a briefly amiable drift,
But poised to leave for some new destination
When all's aboard and you have favorable winds.
Bear the spirit reverently, protect
The quiet, sacred journeys you direct.

Devotion for Night

Crows on the horns of the moon, rapid swerves
Aside by flailing bats who hear each hum,
The old pit bull, whose tragic howl still serves
To prophesy sirens before they come,
Dark motions in darkness escort the deadly night
In dangerous dignity westward; no glowing sun
Will find her, and Asia will hide her from the light
As shadows first hide and then begin to run
Toward the East, where Night will soon arrive,
Cooling down the energies burning away,
Assuring the world the sun will not survive
Her long, slow dance with the furious day.
Her starlit orchestra will play as it played
Before Apollo's bright chariot was made.

Suzannah Lays It on the Table

Just read the plays; you'll find that it's all there.
He built the cathedral of modern literature,
And I made sure that he would never dare
Ignore the voice that kept his drama pure.
He needed a rock to stand on, and that stone
Was me, and he stood, fortunately,
Often isolated, but never alone,
His spirit always in counterpoint with me.
And after Nora, Hedda, and Hilde took the stage
And foolish incompetence threatened his glory—
I didn't mind the girls; my jealous outrage
Arose from the threat to Ibsen's epic story—
I killed him. He knew there never would be
A more Ibsenian woman than me.

Hesitation Galvanizes the Speed of Light

What you were saying to me a while ago
As the sun crawled up and spread his shrouds
And tied his threadbare necktie for the show—
Not expecting enthusiastic crowds,
But hoping someone with brains might drop in—
Was what you said when Moses stopped the sun
To fix the match so his home team would win,
But when that urgent whispering was done,
The words, erased by gentle tongues of smoke,
Flew sideways from that moment, getting here
Just before we did; they tremulously broke
The red orb's speed record, and now I hear
Some of the words you wanted then to say:
Never say good-bye, at least not today.

Letter from a Hittite Librarian

O future scribe, my hieroglyphs bypass
Authority of these divinities
Inflated by the desperate flight
Of wisdom from their portly brains.
I wink at you from dead centuries,
And you may quote my treason now,
If it helps you cope with bullying fools.

The Plane Home from the Ibsen Festival

As confounding as confusion of the elements,
These poisonous minerals block the way
To perfection, hashing together sense and nonsense,
Foolishness, insight, mad hope gone astray,
Anxious disappointment's dull negation,
A kind of biting arrogance alternately
Disdaining all in virtuous indignation
Then groveling, supplicating shamelessly.
But awareness grows, though hidden carefully
As this eccentric three-ring circus rages,
Becoming bitter passion to be free,
So, when the tigers go back to their cages,
A wisdom remains, bought unspeakably,
An antidote to the poison undoing me.

At Chichén Itzá, Thinking of *King Lear*

Watch the light on that moving target change.
The Mayas carved that flickering alteration
In stone, but now the magic concentration
Of geometric force, disturbing and strange,
Has itself escaped where deadly time tiptoes.
Eclipsed in dark hope's cosmic convulsion
And paralyzed by chivalric compulsion
These knights stand at the tragedy's close
As if a miraculous beam of sudden light
Could transform their annihilation
Into a savage, sensible salvation
Less devoid of reason, bereft of right.
The changing reflection that we clearly see
Vanishes irreversibly.

A Damn Good Price on Determinism

Those yapping sparrows scrapping for crumbs
Are tracing the thread of determinism that comes
And threads away, knotted with unknown lines
Twisted by witches into tough, coarse twines.
If you are determined to become proficient
In tracing such lines to their old sources,
May your determination be insufficient
To ruin your mind on irrelevant forces.
Those unknown threads make all the net
As mysterious as those which must restrain,
And from whose limits, irrevocably set,
We merrily pretend to recoil in vain.
Our ties tell of liberty, and we must decide
On the tethers with which we will be finally tied.

The Stone Pyramid in the Rain Forest

Concentric squares declare this blurry joke
Is part of the jungle joke we fail to get,
Grinning and shuffling our nimble nerves to set
Poses for the skeletons who woke
Smiling at our blinding *savoir faire,*
Snappy comebacks, and faraway looks
Into the camera, stuff of golden books,
Stuff of handsome dreams no longer there.
Comb back that snaky hair, and fix your eyes—
Though they aren't broken—what? never mind!—
Upon the solidest fantasy you find
Here where these boxes within boxes rise
To show the always-hovering frigate bird
How in the beginning flies this final word.

The Thracian Rider Is Doomed to Moonlight

Artemis of slippery rocks, O power
Of mesquite, O night, O resonant night
Of owls and tricky rapids, in this hour
Guide my faithful warhorse aright
In this crossing of this magic stream,
Where the ghosts of ancient rattlesnakes
Arise a moment from their deathly dream
To view the crossing an intruder makes.
Thus splashing splashlessly, now I ride,
Saluting the river with my brazen spear,
Across through the shallows to the western side,
To Mexico. Moonglow is strong, but sunrise is near,
And here I will abide when darkness is gone
Awaiting the impulse which will impel me on.

Just one game plays out at no remove
From reality, and its rules both produce
And require defiance of traps that prove
What you are. You must somehow turn loose
Of love's numerous and bogus avatars,
Of pride's super-subtle, invidious claims,
And all false illusions, from Hell to the stars,
As the clock steals vigor, and all the other games
Clamor for attention. But I have arrived
And crossed this river, one dragon slain
In Bulgaria, the battles I survived
Having cleared my soul of useless pain.
And now, freed from compulsion of choice,
I listen for orders from an inward voice.

Last night I met a perished knight at arms
Wandering feebly down the murmuring stream,
And we spoke awhile of debilitating charms
That lurk malignantly in hope and dream.
Death had relieved him of all but regret,
He smiled, his eyes unseen in the ghostly shade,
But hoarsely whispered then that to forget

He'd instantly take agony in trade,
And he reached forth to me his bony hand,
And I pronounced forthwith the living curse,
And he was gone with that crushing command
That the dead must obey and none can reverse.
And the waterfall echoes its perpetual sighs
And I stand watch here silent at moon-rise.

.

Mona Lisa and the Marlboro Man

Not knowing if wisdom would impulsively fly
Or if it dragged its feet when impulse flared,
She had to make the call and suddenly try
To do what an immortal would have dared,
An Aphrodite, ascending in a flying cart
Drawn by fifty gurgling pigeons at a speed
Which matched the speed of her own matchless heart
And the heartbreaking glory of her need.
Later, back in Laredo, she would say
She didn't know why she'd taken off that way,
Smiling with satisfaction, recalling when
Her best moments flew by delightfully then.

He didn't want anyone saying, "Oh.
This is how I feel," but people do
Say that, and he said it, sometimes, too,
In unguarded moments, and he would show
How he felt, displaying great disdain
As he lit his pipe, blew blue smoke forth
Delivering himself from aesthetic pain
Incurred by foolish ideas from the North,
And, nodding slightly to appreciate
A tolerable turn of phrase which he
Thought suggested some brain activity,
He let his tobacco counter-obfuscate
Suspicious overflows of raw emotion
Which threatened to undermine devotion.

To the Daughter of Light

It was closed when we got there, daughter of light,
But disappointments pass like strangers' frowns,
And the trip was worth it. Remember the long night
Driving through West Texas? No cars or towns
For almost forever, we thought, a dim-lit zone
Where astonished stars stared benevolently
At two lost children driving steadily on
As fuel ran low, murmuring confidently
Of hopes ahead and visions vague but strong,
Moving toward hard labor and the final fact:
The shortest distance between two hearts is long
But negotiable, once a code is cracked,
And a door is opened painfully at last
On liberating future and grasping past.

Wherever in this vastness some little asteroid
Coasts quietly at speed, light fluctuating
Along its cold, bleak flanks, a thought in the void,
Be clear that its schedule concedes no waiting
And that when it arrives at last you'll pay
All debts at once for good, as will we all,
And the stars will weep themselves sick that day,
Gargantuan dwarves letting teardrops fall,
To lose your light, your devastating grin,
Your faith in lies and in the god of crime
For the enviable position they've put you in
To await advancement at a favorable time.
And there the sickly, greenish, gibbous moon
Looks away, hopes nothing happens soon.

The Lost Poems of Catullus

The lost poems of Catullus turned up again
In northwest Laredo, Rancho Viejo Drive,
And there they were, all aglow with sin
And burning intelligence. They were fiercely alive
And resonant with bemused electricity,
And they lit up that dusty desert place
With the desperation of futility,
The bitter grace of eloquence in disgrace.
Think a squall of warm Mediterranean rain
Washing these prickly pears and mesquites,
Moistening them inwardly with Roman disdain,
Empowering the graduation it completes
With flowers this land eventually bears
In a sea of stubborn thorns, where no one cares.

Road to Hell Paved with Good Samaritans

You are bleeding to death, poor man, although
Your jaw is a blur of comic domination
And the words squirt forth in a ferocious flow
Of meaningless bullshit, self-congratulation,
Lauded by your lackeys planning to steal
Your throne when this exsanguination
Leaves you as cold as a cold-eyed eel,
No more slimy tricks, no salvation.
Someone with wings should take you aside
And whisper something healing, advocate
The benefits of decency, avoidance of pride,
And the leaks might seal, the reaper might wait.
Can you resist the cruel temptation to kick
The wounded, yourself being deathly sick?

Vision and Code

We need not over-manage confusion.
As potency evolves to expertise
In dealing with futility and illusion
And healing forms of love's beloved disease,
A hard-wired modesty takes the place
Of smugness disguised as objectivity;
As diffidence gradually reforms the face,
The old sophomore earns seniority.
The code spirals down inevitably,
In silences and pauses, expirations,
Unreturned calls, unanswered sympathy,
Mistaken glances, mysterious sensations,
And wisdom remains as what has been said
In this code by the voices in the head.

On Ibsen's *Ghosts*

She was not fortunate in any of those to whom
Her love flowed forth, but somehow wounded hope
Survived betrayal, enabled her to cope
With the intimate infamy of masqueraded doom.
With friends like hers, no wonder she felt pain;
With nowhere to hide, alas, that's where she hid.
She put a brave face on everything she did,
Looking for kindness to mollify disdain,
And when the roof falls in, and desolation
Stares her mercilessly in the face,
The actress takes over, a theatrical grace,
In a light mist of mercy, a visitation.
Screaming is strength, once the men are gone,
And hope amounts, then, to being on her own.

The King of Cobwebs Defies His Foes

(by texting himself a sonnet in bed at 5 a.m.)

"I'm not in the habit of making threats, but there will be a letter
about this in the *Times* tomorrow."
—Groucho Marx

Scheming again, scurrilously scheming,
These drowsy thoughts a vague, temporary,
Instinctive, and unnecessary
Exercise—obnoxious word—in dreaming...
Those who cannot lie successfully
Must hope the truth convenient
To mask the indirection of intent
As well as sly duplicity.
Have you not heard how hence he hurled—
His fury unleashed like Judgment Day
Against all trivia in his way—
Many a mortal sonnet at the world?
My curse on those who dare run down
This Jupiteran rage and wispy crown.

R.W. Haynes, Professor of English at Texas A&M International University, has published poetry in many journals in the United States and in other countries. As an academic scholar, he specializes in British Renaissance literature, and he has also taught extensively in such areas as medieval thought, Southern literature, classical poetry, and writing. Since 1992, he has offered regular graduate and undergraduate courses in Shakespeare, as well as seminars in Ibsen, Chaucer, Spenser, rhetoric, and other topics. In 2004, Haynes met Texas playwright/screenwriter Horton Foote and has since become a leading scholar of that author's remarkable *oeuvre,* publishing a book on Foote's plays in 2010 and editing a collection of essays on his works in 2016. In 2016, Haynes received the SCMLA Poetry Award ($500) at the South Central Modern Language Association Conference. He also writes plays and fiction.